THE BOOK OF

THE BOOK OF

INDIA'S
ANCIENT BOOK
OF PROPHECY

Swami Kriyananda

CRYSTAL CLARITY PUBLISHERS
Commerce, California

CRYSTAL CLARITY PUBLISHERS
1123 Goodrich Blvd. | Commerce, California
crystalclarity.com | clarity@crystalclarity.com
800.424.1055

ISBN 978-1-56589-056-5 (print)
ISBN 978-1-56589-643-7 (e-book)
Library of Congress Cataloging-in-Publication Data:
  2023039187 (print) | 2023039188 (ebook)

Contents

Foreword

*M*ANY CULTURES HAVE TAUGHT THAT our planet passes through a series of "astrological ages" that influence the overall consciousness of mankind. In ancient Greece these ages were called the Gold, Silver, Bronze, and Iron Ages. India, a land with a spiritual tradition going back thousands of years, has its own version of these world ages: the *yugas.* Satya Yuga is the age of truth, when all of humanity is uplifted spiritually. Kali Yuga is the age of darkness, when materialism is most pronounced. Between these two extremes are the second and third ages, called Dwapara and Treta Yugas. It is said that in Dwapara Yuga mankind will gradually overcome the limitation of space as a delusion. In Treta Yuga the limitation of time will be transcended.

These statements might sound rather preposterous to the scientifically minded. One phenomenon, in India, that may open one's mind to possibilities beyond scientific knowledge is *The Book of Bhrigu*, known in that country as the *Bhrigu Samhita*. It consists of libraries of pages, each with information, often quite detailed, about people's lives, that apparently were written before they were ever born. This work is attributed to an ancient sage, Bhrigu, and perhaps also to his disciples.

In this book by Swami Kriyananda you will read remarkable passages from this mysterious ***Bhrigu Samhita***. Swamiji, a direct disciple of the great Indian master Paramhansa Yogananda, and an internationally known spiritual teacher and author himself, was well qualified to investigate this intriguing subject. Swamiji was both intuitive and scientific. When he went to the ***Bhrigu Samhita*** and found that there was a reading for him, he was fascinated. Afterward, wanting to make sure that what he'd seen was genuine, he had the paper and ink tested and verified that the page was older than he was.

The Bhrigu reading for Swamiji was strikingly detailed and accurate. And it was written before his birth! How can this be explained? Conventional astrology makes a horoscope for the moment of birth and then can give information about the life to come.

The *Bhrigu Samhita* probably makes use of astrology, but is also beyond it. It appears to be a source of knowledge that transcends time as it is currently understood. Indeed, it seems likely to have its origins in Treta Yuga, when the consciousness of man can penetrate through time. The last Treta Yuga ended approximately 5,000 years ago. Evidently, for a spiritual master like Bhrigu that was only a moment ago!

Swami Kriyananda has opened a door for us: affording a glimpse into the mystery of *Bhrigu Samhita*, and the hint it gives us that time is not what it seems. Enjoy!

Drupada Macdonald, astrologer
September 2023

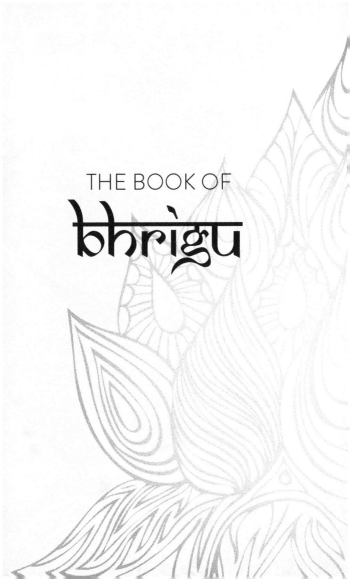

THE BOOK OF
bhrigu

i

"*H*AVE YOU EVER HEARD OF BHRIGU?" Raja Mrigendra Singh's voice carried a note of suppressed excitement.

It was in that eternally fascinating country, India, in the town of Patiala, Punjab. The date was November 29, 1959. My questioner, a local prince, had come to visit me at my temporary residence on Press Road. Tall, of striking features, smartly turbaned after the custom of the Sikhs, his eyes expressive of a character in which strength and kindness were pleasingly blended: I had felt instantly attracted to this man from the moment I had first seen him.

Raja Mrigendra Singh and Pandit Bhagat Ram stand outside the latter's house on Gaushala Road, in Barnala. The pandit is holding the page from Bhrigu's book on which was found recorded the author's life. The brittleness of the paper may be seen from the fact that in handling it a piece has broken off at the lower-left-hand corner of the page.

"Bhrigu?" I echoed my friend's query somewhat uncertainly.

"Bhrigu was a noted *rishi* (sage) in ancient India," my guest explained.

Now I remembered. This venerable name appears often in *Puranic* Scriptures. It is also mentioned in the ancient *Bhagavad Gita,* the "Hindu Bible."

My guest continued: "Bhrigu wrote a book. It is thousands of years old. It contains prophecies about the lives of millions of people, many of whom are living today."

I lowered my gaze in sudden embarrassment. How simply preposterous! Even if such a book could be written, how much would it manage to say about "millions of people"?

I cast about for some ground on which to take my friend's comment with suitable seriousness. Then I recalled the prophecies of Nostradamus.

Nostradamus was a seer in medieval France. He wrote in terse quatrains predictions that supposedly covered world events for centuries to come. Everyone seems to agree that these forecasts were remarkable. They were so cryptic, however, that there is little unanimity of opinion on what they actually mean.

Assuming Bhrigu's prophetic book to be genuine—so I concluded—his predictions might be along the same order as those of the French seer: short sentences that could be applied to any number of people by one with enough faith or imagination, or both, to make them fit.

"How long are these prophecies?" I inquired. "A line or two?"

My friend smiled sympathetically at my skepticism. "Most of them fill one or two pages. They are so detailed that there isn't the least doubting that the information given for a person actually refers to him, and to no one else.

"I found myself mentioned in the book," said the raja. "I actually found my own name written there. (And you know, Mrigendra is an unusual name.) My wife's and my father's names also appeared in my reading. My birthplace was given correctly."

The raja went on to tell of a number of other cases where people had found their own lives described in this book. In some instances only their initials had been given. Even these references, he said, were anything but vague.

He told me about a prominent lady of Patiala, Mrs. Gurdial Singh of Tehsil

Road, who had gone to Bhrigu for a reading. Accompanying her was her brother. Any stranger seeing the couple would naturally have assumed them to be man and wife.

They said nothing to the pandit in charge of the book concerning their actual relationship. Yet in her reading it was stated that she had come with her brother.[*]

"But," I expostulated, "how can millions of lives be described in such detail in a single book?"

"Oh, it isn't a bound volume like those of our present age. The books in ancient India consisted of loose leaves tied together into bundles. This 'book' of Bhrigu's is made up of many such bundles. It requires whole rooms to

---

[*] Mrs. Singh afterwards corroborated this story for me personally.

house it. There are several portions of it in various parts of the country. It is known as the *Bhrigu Samhita.*

"Of course," he added, "not all these portions are equally reliable. There are persons, in fact, who only pretend to have possession of Bhrigu's book, but who read from something quite different."

"I can imagine!" In my mind's eye I could picture the scores of penurious fortunetellers I had seen in the streets of India's crowded cities. What an edge it would give them over their competitors if they could claim exclusive possession of part of so marvelous an ancient document as this!

"These fake custodians of the *Bhrigu Samhita* daren't, of course, let you examine their pages," my friend continued. "They will put you off with some pretext or other—perhaps that the readings are too sacred to be passed about, or that they are written in a style which only those with special training can decipher. Of course, frauds will tell you nothing that they couldn't have found out about you during the course of your conversation with them. Beyond that, they will be studiedly vague."

"But if there are frauds," I suggested, "some of them will doubtless be better at this 'art' than others. So how can one be perfectly sure of *any* of them?"

"The final proof, of course, rests in the results. I've searched far and wide for genuine *Samhitas*. I'm satisfied that I've found at least one, and possible two or three.

"In this one particularly, there are none of the disadvantages one so commonly encounters. The pandit allows you to examine your page carefully. He has even permitted me to take mine home and get a photostatic copy made of it (though this is a privilege he seldom grants anyone). A convincing factor, also, is the time it takes him to locate a page. He rarely has any way of knowing in advance who will be coming to him. Yet, unlike other readers I have met, he finds one's reading *on the spot*. There is no opportunity for him to write it out after having come to know you. And I am impressed by the fact that his fee is low. He cannot be using the book to become rich.

"Finally, of course, many of his predictions have come true."

"Where is this portion that you say you've found?" I inquired.

"It is in a small town called Barnala, only sixty miles from here. Would you like to go there?"

The raja seemed quite in earnest. But could such an exotic manuscript *possibly* be authentic? I struggled to apply my friend's strange story to what I knew of India's spiritual teachings.

The Hindu scriptures, I recalled, state that time is a mental concept. In their view, life may be compared to a book, in that we are conscious of its unfolding events only as we pass from page to page. The pages are turned for us. Could we ourselves hold the book, we would be able to look ahead and read what is written in later chapters. Essentially, there is no past, present, and future. These all exist simultaneously. But for practical purposes we may say that the present is where the book is presently opened.

A natural question arises: What about free will? If the future is already determined for us, doesn't this make us all just puppets in the hands of fate?

Not so, say the ancient teachings. For it is man himself who determines how his role shall read. The operative principle is the law of cause and effect, known in India as the law of Karma.

Even in creations by human artists whimsical fate is ruled out. Any truly competent author lets his characters work out their own destinies. He may see clearly, before he ever writes the first page of a novel, all that must occur to them as the story unfolds. But his book always in a sense "writes itself." He will not force his creations to act "out of character" to suit the predilections of his own nature. Nor will he impose on his characters destinies that they haven't themselves in some way invited.

If God did not know the entire future of His universe and of all its creatures, He would not be omniscient. Foreknowledge need not contradict the doctrine of free will. The human race determines its future by what it *is*, not by what some Higher Being decrees it shall be.

Countless persons have had uncanny feelings—and others, vivid dreams—that something unexpected was going to happen. And it did actually come to pass. Great prophets may be considered simply to have perfected this natural power, infrequently expressed in the lives of ordinary men. In other words, sages have attuned themselves more exactly to the omniscience of God.

I began to wonder seriously, as I struggled through this philosophical hinterland, whether Bhrigu could not, just possibly, have written such an improbable book as this *Samhita*. If he had, I thought, what impressive support it would give to the claim of modern Hindus that their ancient wisdom was as realistic, in its own way, as our twentieth-century sciences! The matter seemed well worth the small effort of investigation.

"How can I get to Barnala?" I asked my friend.

"I am going there tomorrow morning," he replied. "I came here today to ask you if you wouldn't like to come along."

II

*T*HE **FOLLOWING MORNING** I **WAS** midway through a quick breakfast when the raja's car entered our driveway. Three tall young men stepped out, all of them neatly turbaned. Raja Mrigendra introduced me to two of his brothers.

Soon we were bumping over the narrow washboard of a road that leads to Barnala.

We passed through vast estates belonging to the Maharaja of Patiala. Raja Mrigendra is a brother of this famous onetime ruler, who, after the liberation of India, won the admiration and gratitude of the whole country for his sponsorship of the abolishment of many princely states in favor of national unity.

"Tell me," I said as our conversation reverted to Bhrigu, "how does the pandit find a correct page, out of so many?"

"There are two ways to approach the book," Raja Mrigendra replied. "One is to give the pandit your birth horoscope. The other, and simpler, method is to ask Bhrigu a question. In the latter case, the pandit prepares a chart giving the positions of the planets at the very moment when you asked your question. He then looks in the *Samhita* for a chart exactly corresponding to the one he has prepared. Bhrigu knew that on just such-and-such a day, at such-and-such a time, a particular individual would come before his book and ask a particular question.

"I should explain that astrology has little to do with these readings," the raja added. "The horoscopes are primarily a means of locating the correct pages.

"To find a page by means of the birth horoscope is a task that requires, sometimes, days. But to get an answer to a question is a relatively simple matter. The pandit has a certain method whereby he can quickly tell in which bundle your answer will be, if there *is* an answer.

"Many people, I should warn you, find nothing at all for themselves. There may be nothing there for you. But it is quite possible that there will at least be something found for *someone* while we are there today.

"One day," the raja continued, "the pandit prepared a horoscope for a woman who had asked a question. He found that he had written two of the numbers in the chart incorrectly. He crossed them out and wrote down the right figures. When the page was located, it was found that the same two numbers had been written in wrongly by Bhrigu, crossed out, then entered correctly!

"If you ask a question, you are not required to tell the pandit what you have asked. You ask it mentally only. But when an answer is found it will be in detail. Sometimes many specific questions are answered in a single reading.

"The pandit himself," my friend concluded, "is just an ordinary person who happens to be in possession of an extraordinary book. He does nothing for you except locate the right leaf and read it out to you."

Raja Mrigendra had brought along

two typewriters, one with English characters for my benefit, and the other for typing out in Hindi any answers received by him or his brothers.

One reason the three brothers were coming on this occasion was to type out a reading that one of them, a younger brother of my friend, had received a few days earlier. Something in Bhrigu's forecast evidently had this young man not a little worried. He had been gazing glumly out of the car window most of the way.

Referring to his brother's distress, Raja Mrigendra said, "Bhrigu never tells you anything negative unless there is some positive good that may come of the revelation. He has warned my brother of something serious that could happen to him, but he has also suggested a way out of the predicament.

"Bhrigu also sometimes scolds people for grave faults," he added, "if gentler treatment isn't likely to penetrate their thick shells of egotism. Usually the readings are the very essence of tact. Sometimes, however, they can be very blunt.

"Once a woman went to Barnala with her family. She was one of those persons whose practice it is to condemn the petty faults of everyone around them. Herself she set up self-righteously before the world as a model of virtue.

"The pandit found a page for her and started to read it out. It is his usual practice, because he has only a small house, to read out the pages in the same room where visitors gather. He makes an exception when he sees that a reading contains information that the subject is likely to want kept confidential.

While reading this woman's page out to her, he suddenly stopped. 'If you don't mind,' he continued, 'I would prefer to read the following passage to you privately.'

"There were others in the room besides her family. She must have felt that by agreeing to the pandit's request she would lose face before them. Of course, it was her guilty conscience that prompted her, otherwise why should she think that just because a passage was confidential it was necessarily damning? But evidently she couldn't believe that Bhrigu knew enough about her to be embarrassingly specific. She rashly instructed the pandit to continue reading in the presence of them all.

"Again he requested her, this time pleadingly. But to no avail.

"Well, he finally began, in an uneasy tone of voice, to read out the next passage. In it were described in harrowing detail her secret vices. The reading mentioned one man by name, saying that for years she had been having illicit relations with him. It said that she had had one of her children by him, not by her husband. Both the man and the child were present in the room with her. The man was a trusted friend of the family. Bhrigu went on to scold the woman in scathing terms for her hypocrisy.

"It was a most distressing episode. What was there to say? The child even looked like the man described by Bhrigu as his father. But perhaps the shock of this relentless exposure helped the woman as nothing else could have done."

The raja continued: "Numerous persons go to the *Bhrigu Samhita* in

Barnala. Very few are reproved by Bhrigu for their weaknesses, moral or otherwise. Bhrigu was a man of God. Like all saints, he preferred encouraging people in their virtues to condemning them for their faults."

The highway to Barnala, though paved, was so uneven it made conversation difficult. The country on both sides of us was mostly flat and uninteresting. Broad, semiarid fields made way occasionally, as if grudgingly, for tiny, poor villages that clung piteously to the roadside. The people living here seemed to eke out only a bare subsistence from the soil.

I thought sadly of the need of Indian villages for Western technical skills.

And then I found myself meditating on the peace reflected in the faces of so many of the villagers. Have not they, too, something tangible and worthwhile to offer to us in the West? Can we, for all our glory, honestly say that we have found fulfillment—lacking, as most of us do, contentment and a peaceful heart?

The harsh, dry countryside around us, seemingly resentful of man's intrusion, finally surrendered to the swaggering conquest of the little, bustling town of Barnala. We bounced through narrow streets until we reached Gaushala Road.

Here, in a typical Indian home of modest proportions, lives Pandit Bhagat Ram, custodian of the *Bhrigu Samhita.*

It was with some effort that we pulled ourselves out of the car, our bodies stiff with protest at the jolting they had received on the way.

Proceeding down a narrow lane, we soon came to an unimpressive doorway and stood before it while the raja knocked. After some minutes a servant came out. Smiling apologetically, he informed us that the pandit had gone to the bazar, but would be back shortly. It was still early, and working hours had not yet started. The servant invited us in to wait. Removing our shoes, we entered the interview room and sat cross-legged on the padded floor-covering.

There was no furniture here. None was expected. Chairs and tables are the rankest superfluities where people are content to sit on the floor.

While we waited for the pandit to come, I pointed to a simple sign in Hindi characters on one of the walls. In answer to my unspoken question, a stranger, who had entered the room shortly after us, said:

"It is a sort of advertisement, telling people that in the *Bhrigu Samhita* they will find information relating to three incarnations: past, present, and future."

A strange place to advertise, I thought—*inside* the house! But apparently the *Samhita* requires no publicity. Already the room was beginning to fill up with people anxious to secure readings for themselves. They squatted quietly in hopeful expectation, like patients in a doctor's parlor.

It would be digressing from our story here to enter into a serious discussion of transmigration of souls. The point may be considered, however, that if the *Bhrigu Samhita* is proved to be genuine it will add considerable weight to the case for this doctrine.

"Speaking of reincarnation," Raja Mrigendra remarked, "there was a woman in here when I first came who was told by Bhrigu that in her last life she lived in Patal-Desh,* in the town of 'Wash-ing-ton.' In Sanskrit characters this ancient reading actually spelled out the sounds of the name!"

There were by my side a few loose pages of the *Bhrigu Samhita.* I examined them. They seemed old, I thought—yet not so ancient as I had expected.

"This is only a copy of the original," someone explained to me. "The actual book written by Bhrigu is believed to be hidden somewhere in Tibet."

The pandit finally entered the room apologizing for having kept us waiting.

---

* This name appears often in ancient Sanskrit writings. It is now usually taken to be a reference to America. *Patal* means "underneath"; *desh* means "country"—"The country on the under, or opposite, side of the world." The American continents do contain striking indications that the ancient Indian culture may have penetrated to this side of our planet.

We stood up to greet him. He welcomed Raja Mrigendra first, with a trace of deference in his manner for his visitor's rank. Next he was introduced to me.

The pandit's face and bearing impressed me favorably. I was sorry to find that he spoke no English. Others had to translate our conversation, which took time and probably left many thoughts uncommunicated. Nevertheless, we were able to converse together with a fair degree of fluency.

I was pleased with what seemed to me to be his sincerity and humility. I felt reassured that, whether the book was true or false, this man at least believed in it implicitly.

A visitor addressed him as if speaking to a sage. Immediately the pandit placed the palms of his hands supplicatingly together and said, "Please,

I am no one. It is the book alone that deserves your respect. I only read to you from its pages."

On learning that I am an American, the pandit smiled. "There was an American from Texas who came here some time ago," he told me. "He had been brought by a friend, but knew nothing about Bhrigu. I found a page for him and began reading out what was written on it. Halfway through the reading the man leaped to his feet. 'This place is haunted!' he shouted, running from the room."

I assured the pandit with a smile that no matter what he found for me, I would hear it out bravely to the end.

A part of the *Bhrigu Samhita* in Barnala. The pages are wrapped carefully into bundles, each of which is numbered for identification.

III

*T*HE TIME CAME AT LAST TO SEE whether there was a reading for me.

I had decided on the type of reading that answers questions. But I kept to myself what my questions were.

The pandit drew up a planetary chart according to the exact minute when I had asked him to seek a page for me. After studying the chart for a time and making several other reckonings, he said, "Yes, there should be a reading for you today." He added, "It ought to be in bundle 52."

So saying, he left the room. Two minutes later he returned, carrying a heavy package wrapped carefully in cloth. Setting it on the floor, he opened it and took out a stack of loose pages, yellowed with age.

"Your reading should be among these," he said.

To save time, the pandit split the stack into thirds. He gave one stack to me, one to Raja Mrigendra, and kept one himself, instructing us to look for a card with a planetary chart similar to the one he had drawn up.

"Sometimes," he said, "if my watch is a little fast or slow, there will be a slight difference between Bhrigu's chart and the one I have made. I use Bhrigu to set my watch correctly!"

We went carefully through our respective stacks. I had to be a little more cautious than the others, because the numerical figures were foreign to me.

Suddenly I thought I recognized a few faded numbers. I held up the page for the pandit's inspection. He compared the two diagrams carefully. They were exactly alike.

Taking the page, the pandit began to read. Raja Mrigendra translated for me. This is what I heard:

"AUM. Sri Shukra (the son of Bhrigu) said: 'In the dark half of the month of *Margshirsh*, on a Monday of the *Amavasya*, at eight *ghatis* and thirty *palls*,* what is this combination of planets called, and what is the reading of the person who asks a question at this time? What was his last incarnation, and what thoughts has he in his mind on this occasion?'

"Sri Bhrigu answered: 'O Shukra, this planetary combination is known as

* By our reckoning it was November 30, 1959, at about 10:30 a.m.

"**Guruka Yoga**." According to it the person concerned was born in his last life in the western part of Bharat (India), in a town the name of which begins with the letter K. This city is now ruled by the **Yavans**,* and is the capital of their country.

"'This *jiva* (individual soul) was born into the **Arrura** branch (or **vansha**) of the **Kshatriya** caste. His family was well-to-do. His name was Pujar Das. He was an **astik** (one having faith in the **Vedas**) and a religious person. . . .

"'After passing years (in that place), he and his wife went together on a pilgrimage. Ultimately their travels took them to the desert, where they visited the **ashram** (hermitage) of the sage

---

* This ancient name signified the people living in or near Persia, or coming from that general region. The *Yavans* in latter-day India would be the Moslems. Bhrigu was evidently referring to Karachi, the capital of modern Pakistan.

Kapila. . . . Here this person remained for many years.'"

The story took Pujar Das to the time of his death. I have given only such excerpts as may perhaps be of interest to others, particularly from the standpoint of glimpsing the style in which the *Bhrigu Samhita* was written.

The account then continued: "'In this life, after much traveling, he has arrived in my presence, having been coaxed to come here by one of my devotees, a member of a royal family.'"

I swallowed hard. This part, at least, applied: the extensive traveling; the fact of my having come only after being coaxed; Mrigendra's rank.

"'This person's name,'" the pandit continued, "'is Kriyananda'"!

Stunned, I took the card and passed it to several persons in the room who had come in hope of finding readings for themselves, and who said they were familiar with Sanskrit characters. They all confirmed that it did in fact say Kriyananda. This name is, so far as I know, unique.

The pandit took the page again and continued reading. The account defined correctly the type of spiritual discipline I follow; it mentioned that I had been lecturing in foreign countries; it gave various facts of a personal nature, and made certain predictions. At least as far as the known facts of this life went, the reading was correct.

Bhrigu also answered specifically the questions I had put to him mentally.

As regards my supposed last incarnation, I have at least the following facts to ponder: In this life I never glimpsed a desert until I grew up. Yet the first desert I ever knew, at the age of twenty-two, seemed strangely familiar to me; more than once I mentioned to others that I felt more at home there than anywhere else on earth. Why this sudden love for bare sand and tumbleweed? I had been accustomed to rich greenery, flower gardens, and mountain slopes. Again, the Hindu scriptures exercised an immediate and unusual appeal for me the day when, as a young man, I first read a few excerpts from them in a book called *The Short World Bible.* My religious upbringing had been orthodox: Episcopalian, mostly. I can think of no influence in this life that would explain either of these spontaneous interests. Doesn't Bhrigu's account offer an intriguing answer?

(It might be of interest here to add that I obtained another reading a few months later, from another portion of the **Bhrigu Samhita**. In this one a much earlier incarnation was described—because, Bhrigu explained, he had already told me ("in my *Yoga Valli*") about my *last* life. My place of birth in this life was correctly given, though misspelled: Rumania was written, "Rumanake." The reading stated that my father named me "James"—my actual first name at baptism. The reading said that I have lived in America. It gave my monastic name, Kriyananda. A fact was brought out about my family that I myself did not know, but that I was able to verify some months later after my return to America. This reading made a number of unexpected predictions, several of which have already since come true.)

Bhagat Ram's usual fee for finding

a page and translating it is Rupees 21, which comes to a little over four American dollars. In my case he refused payment because I am a monk.

A portion of a reading received by the author. The
chart indicates the time at which he requested that
the reading be sought for him. Circled at the top is
his name, Kriyananda, in Sanskrit characters.

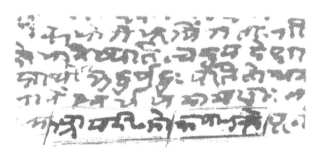

Another portion of the same reading as No. 4. Here are circled the names, *America* and *Rumanake*, transliterated in Sanskrit characters. The first country is, as the reading states, the place where the author has lived. The second (Rumania) is where he was born (of American parents).

IV

*T*HE PANDIT BEGAN TO TELL ME A FEW
stories about the *Samhita*. There
was a yogi, he said, who lived far out in
the jungle, passing his days in meditation. One night he had a dream of Bhrigu,
as a result of which he came to Barnala
to consult the *Bhrigu Samhita*. A reading
was found for him in which it was written: "This person has had a vision of me.
That is why he has come to this place."

The story of how the pandit came
into possession of this book is a fascinating one.

As a boy he was subject to many
diseases. While he was still very young,
he lost his parents and passed years in

desperate poverty. Shortly before he attained manhood he was taken by a friend to a portion of the **Bhrigu Samhita**.

A page was found for him. On it was written: "In your last life you were a custodian of my book. But you misused your position, taking for yourself offerings that people had intended for me, to be used for charity. That is why you have encountered suffering in this life. But there is also much goodness in you, and if you will give in charity a certain large sum (which Bhrigu specified) it will be possible to erase the sins of your past life. In this case you will return to your former post.

"Some years hence you will be traveling in another place, and will come across an old woman who has possession of my **Samhita**. She will give it to you, and you will once again be my custodian."

The pandit was able with time and effort to make the required gift. Some years later he was traveling in Punjab, and came to Barnala with a friend. Here someone happened to tell him of an old woman in their present neighborhood who had inherited an ancient unidentified manuscript.

Bhagat Ram concealed his excitement. Requesting his traveling companion to go on without him, he explained that he himself had decided to settle in Barnala for awhile. After the departure of his friend, he went to the woman's house and offered to help her gratuitously with her housework.

The woman was grateful, naturally. She was alone, and too old to work about the house without difficulty. Bhagat Ram easily succeeded in ingratiating himself with her. In return for his services she gave him, on his request, a few pages of her book. It proved to be indeed the *Bhrigu Samhita*!

But the old woman, though no scholar, had her fair share of peasant cunning. When she realized how much the book meant to this young man, she feared that if she gave him the whole of it his services to her might cease! She therefore released to him only parts of it at a time, with the understanding that at her death he might have it all. So far as I know, she is still alive, and the greater portion of the manuscript remains in her home. The pandit has access to it even there, however, and may take from it any page he requires.

Pandit Bhagat Ram has had the book now fourteen years. During the early days of his custodianship of it he decided that it was not well organized. He set about arranging the pages in a manner that better suited him. But he encountered unexpected difficulties. Finally it occurred to him to consult Bhrigu in the matter. In the *Samhita* he found the explanation:

"My reader thinks he knows better than I do how my book should be arranged. But he fails to understand that I have put it in its present order for a purpose, and that I do not wish this order to be changed. Let him return the pages to their former places." Needless to say, the pandit hastily complied with the instruction.

Bhagat Ram himself often consults the *Samhita*. As our conversation shifted temporarily to America, he told me, "Bhrigu has told me I shall go there some day."

Tales of Bhrigu's foreknowledge never cease to stagger the imagination. One day Raja Mrigendra was in Barnala listening to a reading of his. Halfway through it, Bhrigu said, "While this is being read, two of this person's brothers will enter the room." The raja had come from Patiala by car, without the slightest knowledge that two of his brothers also wanted to come that day. They came separately, by train. Just as this passage was being read out, they entered the room.

Mata Brahma Jyoti, known in religious circles
in New Delhi, is a Hindu *sannyasini*, or nun. She
often stays at the home of K. G. Khosla, 11 Prithvi
Raj Road, where a Bhrigu pandit comes occasionally to give readings. Mataji, as this *sannyasini* is
generally called, wears the traditional flame-color
of renunciation. She entertains a deep faith in the
Bhrigu Samhita.

V

IT WAS AN amazing story. But wasn't
it *too* amazing? I wanted to know if
there were any hidden loopholes.

I took a later reading to Connaught
Circus, the shopping center of New
Delhi, and had a photostatic copy made
of it. While in the capital I was able to
check the reading with several Sanskrit
scholars, and thereby to make certain
that nothing had been read by the pandit beyond what was actually written.
As a matter of fact, I discovered that in
reading the page he had left out several
lines by mistake.

I took the page to the laboratory of
the National Archives of India. There

I inquired whether there were any means of ascertaining the approximate date of the writing. The paper was yellowed and brittle, apparently with age. The writing looked faded. Nevertheless, I thought, there might be some method of achieving such effects artificially.

The laboratory technicians told me that they had no way of telling the age of either the paper or the ink. By certain chemical processes, they said, it is possible to treat new paper and make it look old. And of course, they added, ink can easily be made to look faded.

"But haven't you some sort of carbon processes or something?" I inquired, admittedly ignorant of these esoteric procedures. (It still astonishes me that in this age of science these men could offer no certain proof of the age of this

manuscript.) They repeated that they
knew of no method to accomplish what
I wanted.

"Is there any way," I then asked,
"that you can tell whether this writing is more than a month old?" The
writing *was*, after all, said to be only
a copy of the original. It might well
be a copy of a copy. I had known this
Bhrigu pandit less than two weeks.
Even if the reading had been fairly
recently copied, I thought, so long as
it was definitely older than one month
I might be at least somewhat satisfied
as to its authenticity.

"We can certainly test it for such
a short period of time as one month,"
the technicians replied. "If the writing
is comparatively recent, the ink won't
have had time yet to become 'set' in
the paper."

After testing the ink they said that it was well set. "The writing is positively much older than a month," they assured me.

Next I took the page to the Archeological Department of India. On my request, I was allowed to see the Director of the Department, Dr. A. Ghosh. This gentleman, a Bengali of dignified mien, studied the document not only from the standpoint of its general appearance, but also from that of the style of the handwriting.

"Well," he announced after a careful perusal, "it isn't very old."

"How old would that imply?" I asked him.

"I would estimate only about a hundred or a hundred and fifty years."

"Please be so kind as to tell me one thing more," I said. "Can you see whether the name, Kriyananda, appears anywhere in this section?" I pointed out to him approximately where, if at all, my name would appear.

He studied that section briefly, then said, "Yes, here it is. 'Kriyananda.' I must say, it is a most unusual name." He added, "This looks like Bhrigu. Is it?"

Champions of the *Bhrigu Samhita* assure me confidently that it is never incorrect. Sometimes, they admit, mistakes do occur in the copying of a particular reading from the original. But these instances, they insist, are exceedingly rare.

I learned of one man who was told in a portion of the *Bhrigu Samhita* in Banaras that five years later he would die. He lived in dread of the day. After five years had passed, he was still very much alive. He lost all faith in Bhrigu.

Much later he happened upon another portion of the *Samhita* elsewhere. On an impulse he decided to ask Bhrigu why the Banaras prediction had failed. A reading was found for him. Therein he was told that at the time his previous reading was copied, a line had accidentally been left off the top of a letter. As a result, the meaning had been completely changed. What Bhrigu had originally written was that after five years this person would lose all his property. The accidental omission of a single penstroke had made all the difference between poverty and death!

"And *did* you lose everything at that time?" inquired the pandit.

"It is true, I did!" exclaimed the visitor, struck with wonder and amazement.

I interviewed many persons who had consulted Bhrigu, or who knew others that had done so. The accuracies of his readings continued to be astounding. But gradually a picture emerged of predictions that had failed. I came upon quite a number of such cases. Could *all* these errors, I wondered, be due to the blunders of copiers? Frankly, it didn't seem likely.

At last I met a scholar in Calcutta who had done extensive research on this subject. He told me that the *Bhrigu Samhita* is for the most part (and contrary to what Raja Mrigendra had claimed) based on astrology. He said that this book was not actually written by Bhrigu himself, but by many highly trained pandits on the basis of a science that Bhrigu had anciently worked out. (Hence the application of his name to the entire work.) According to this science, my informant said, it is possible to be reasonably accurate with regard to past happenings from any given point in time, and also with respect to the immediate future, but there is less certainty concerning events in more distant futurity.

The possibility that many persons shared the task of writing this book suggests a solution to a question that had nagged me from the first: How could *one* man ever have found the time to write so much!

If one admits the possibility that astrology *is* a science (and the very subject is taboo in most modern circles), this Calcutta scholar's explanation may serve better than any other to solve some of the basic riddles with which the **Bhrigu Samhita** confronts us. But further research in the matter is needed before any solution is definitely accepted.

Whatever the true explanation, the knowledge that alone could have made this book possible is manifestly so vast, and so vastly **different** from anything known to our modern age, that it merits serious investigation not merely by amateurs like me, but by men who have received careful training in the exacting methods of research.

Doesn't the undertaking hold out a rare promise of scholarly adventure?

VI

$\mathcal{I}$T REMAINS FOR US TO CONSIDER the intrinsic *value* of this book of Bhrigu's. This question will very likely be among the first to have occurred to the thoughtful reader.

If a person can be warned of pitfalls ahead of him on his life's journey, and of how he may avoid them, the forecast may well help him. But if the book is not infallible, any person placing undue faith in it may make grave mistakes in the conduct of his affairs.

Besides this, are there not other serious disadvantages? Is there not, for instance, a danger of one's depending on this book to the extent of losing touch with his own inner guidance and good judgment? Again, a little acquaintance with suprarational phenomena may strengthen one's faith in God, if his faith needs such support; but too great a fascination with the miraculous is certain to lessen one's devotion to higher truths and to God. After all, miracles *are* fascinating. They tend to draw the mind away from a loving relationship with the Creator, by focusing the attention on the more dazzling marvels of His creation.

An excessive concern, moreover, with the past and the future, which may develop if one leans too heavily on this book, may only prevent one from living fully *right now*, in the present tense. It seems to me that this is actually the case with certain people whose lives have become wrapped up in the *Samhita.*

Why, then, with questions dangling over both the accuracy and the inherent usefulness of the *Bhrigu Samhita,* have I written this elaborate account of it? I have done so primarily for the very reason that drew me, experimentally, to Barnala in the first place: I see in this ancient manuscript concrete evidence that India's hoary wisdom was based on a practical, definite knowledge of the true nature of things, and not on mere philosophical speculations. And I believe that this evidence will help to open the minds of many Westerners to the mighty culture of which this *Samhita* is only a fragment.

Certainly, whatever the actual origin of this book, it reveals a science and a knowledge that fairly stagger the imagination in this smug age, which boasts that its own mighty achievements are by far the greatest in the whole history of man.

Western scholars tend generally to shelve the profound writings of India's ancient seers under a label of lofty but baseless theories; or to toss them aside as the poetic musings of tenders of cattle. Never having tested those "theories" in their own lives, these learned men consider themselves qualified, by reason of the numerous books they have read, to sit in judgment over the philosophical insight of men who may never have studied Plato, but who have made it their business to learn from the book of life itself.

To submit higher truths to the test of experience is, admittedly, not easy. It requires years of painstaking self-discipline and inner meditative research. But lesser truths are more easily verified, and suggest convincingly that their parent principles might well be *at least* as true.

"Except ye see signs and wonders, ye will not believe." (John 4:48) This account of the prophecies of Bhrigu may have persuaded some readers that the remainder of Indian philosophy also merits their respectful study.

The true teachings of India lie far above the plane of miracles. Divine love, blissful communion with God, a transmuted life of selfless service, humility, and joy—these are the ideals that have kept Indian culture alive and flourishing through the onslaught of countless foreign conquests. And these are the principles through which India will rise again in the future—to become, in very likelihood, one of the beacon lights of brotherhood and peace.

The West today needs India, even as India today needs the West. We Westerners know what gifts we can bestow on others: our scientific and material knowledge, our technical skills. But we are not yet so keenly aware of the priceless riches we can receive from other cultures in return. Awaiting our discovery in India is untold wisdom to live life in the fullest measure of true peace, happiness, and enlightened understanding.

Swami Kriyananda

About the Author

"Swami Kriyananda is a man of wisdom and compassion in action, truly one of the leading lights in the spiritual world today."

—Lama Surya Das, Dzogchen Center, author of
Awakening the Buddha Within

A prolific author, accomplished composer, playwright, and artist, and a world-renowned spiritual teacher, Swami Kriyananda (1926–2013) referred to himself simply as a close disciple of the great God-realized master, Paramhansa Yogananda. He met his guru at the age of twenty-two, and served him during the last four years of the Master's life. He dedicated the rest of his life to sharing Yogananda's teachings throughout the world.

Kriyananda was born in Romania of American parents, and educated in Europe, England, and the United States. Philosophically and artistically inclined from youth, he soon came to question life's meaning and society's values. During a period of intense inward reflection, he discovered Yogananda's *Autobiography of a Yogi,* and immediately traveled three thousand miles from New York to California to meet the Master, who accepted him as a monastic disciple. Yogananda appointed him as the head of the monastery, authorized him to teach and give Kriya initiation in his name, and entrusted him with the missions of writing, teaching, and creating what he called "world brotherhood colonies."

Kriyananda founded the first such community, Ananda Village, in the Sierra Nevada foothills of Northern

California in 1968. Ananda is recognized as one of the most successful intentional communities in the world today. It has served as a model for other such communities that he founded subsequently in the United States, Europe, and India.

Further Explorations

CRYSTAL CLARITY PUBLISHERS

If you enjoyed this title, Crystal Clarity Publishers invites you to deepen your spiritual life through many additional resources based on the teachings of Paramhansa Yogananda. We offer books, e-books, audiobooks, yoga and meditation videos, and a wide variety of inspirational and relaxation music composed by Swami Kriyananda.

See a listing of books below, visit our secure website for a complete online catalog, or place an order for our products.

crystalclarity.com

800.424.1055 | clarity@crystalclarity.com

1123 Goodrich Blvd. | Commerce, CA 90022

ANANDA WORLDWIDE

Crystal Clarity Publishers is the publishing house of Ananda, a worldwide spiritual movement founded by Swami Kriyananda, a direct disciple of Paramhansa Yogananda. Ananda offers resources and support for your spiritual journey through meditation instruction, webinars, online virtual community, email, and chat.

Ananda has more than 150 centers and meditation groups in over 45 countries, offering group guided meditations, classes and teacher training in meditation and yoga, and many other resources.

In addition, Ananda has developed eight residential communities in the US, Europe, and India. Spiritual communities are places where people live together in a spirit of cooperation and friendship, dedicated to a common goal. Spirituality is practiced in all areas of daily life: at school, at work, or in the home. Many Ananda communities offer internships during which one can stay and experience spiritual community firsthand.

For more information about Ananda communities or meditation groups near you, please visit **ananda.org** or call 530.478.7560.

THE EXPANDING LIGHT RETREAT

The Expanding Light is the largest retreat center in the world to share exclusively the teachings of Paramhansa Yogananda. Situated in the Ananda Village community near Nevada City, California, the center offers the opportunity to experience spiritual life in a contemporary ashram setting. The varied, year-round schedule of classes and programs on yoga, meditation, and spiritual practice includes Karma Yoga, personal retreat, spiritual travel, and online learning. Large groups are welcome.

The Ananda School of Yoga & Meditation offers certified yoga, yoga therapist, spiritual counselor, and meditation teacher trainings.

The teaching staff has years of experience practicing Kriya Yoga meditation and all aspects of Paramhansa Yogananda's teachings. You may come for a relaxed personal renewal, participating in ongoing activities as much or as little as you wish. The serene mountain setting, supportive staff, and delicious vegetarian meals provide an ideal environment for a truly meaningful stay, be it a brief respite or an extended spiritual vacation.

For more information, please visit **expandinglight.org** or call 800.346.5350.

ANANDA MEDITATION RETREAT

Set amidst seventy-two acres of beautiful meditation gardens and wild forest in Northern California's Sierra foothills, the Ananda Meditation Retreat is an ideal setting for a rejuvenating, inner experience.

The Meditation Retreat has been a place of deep meditation and sincere devotion for over fifty years. Long before that, the Native American Maidu tribe held this to be sacred land. The beauty and presence of the Divine are tangibly felt by all who visit here.

Studies show that being in nature and using techniques such as forest bathing can significantly reduce stress and blood pressure while strengthening your immune system, concentration, and level of happiness. The Meditation Retreat is the perfect place for quiet immersion in nature.

Plan a personal retreat, enjoy one of the guided retreats, or choose from a variety of programs led by the caring and joyful staff.

For more information or to place your reservation, please visit **meditationretreat.org**, email **meditationretreat@ananda.org**, or call 530.478.7557.

THE BOOK OF BHRIGU AND FREE WILL

A talk by Swami Kriyananda

We long to be free: free from the pressures of work, and from the demands of others. Free to do as we feel inspired. This desire for freedom is one of our deepest drives. We want to captain the ship of our lives, and feel that we are in charge. But wherever we end up, we discover one inescapable problem. We've taken ourselves with us. Our habits and tendencies are so strong, we find ourselves thinking and doing the same things over and over. Even if we could escape our personalities, we are also influenced by the great ocean of humanity around us.

What, then, is freedom? How can it be achieved?

Kriyananda shares here two readings he received in India, written by a saint, Bhrigu, thousands of years ago. These readings, like those given to many others living today, described details of his life with such extraordinarily accuracy that we naturally wonder: Do we have any free will? In answering this question, Kriyananda asks (and answers) two others: Is free will the ability to do anything we want? What is true freedom? He goes on to offer us four essential rules for achieving it.

crystalclarity.com/bhrigutalk

The Original 1946 Unedited Edition
Yogananda's Spiritual Masterpiece

AUTOBIOGRAPHY OF A YOGI
Paramhansa Yogananda

Autobiography of a Yogi is one of the world's most acclaimed spiritual classics, with millions of copies sold. Named one of the Best 100 Spiritual Books of the twentieth century, this book helped launch and continues to inspire a spiritual awakening throughout the Western world.

Yogananda was the first yoga master of India whose mission brought him to settle and teach in the West. His firsthand account of his life experiences in India includes childhood revelations, stories of his visits to saints and masters, and long-secret teachings of yoga and Self-realization that he first made available to the Western reader.

This reprint of the original 1946 edition is free from textual changes made after Yogananda's passing in 1952. This updated edition includes bonus materials: the last chapter that Yogananda wrote in 1951, also without posthumous changes, the eulogy Yogananda wrote for Gandhi, and a new foreword and afterword by Swami Kriyananda, one of Yogananda's close, direct disciples.

Also available in Spanish and Hindi
from Crystal Clarity Publishers.

SCIENTIFIC HEALING AFFIRMATIONS
Paramhansa Yogananda

Yogananda's 1924 classic, reprinted here, is a pioneering work in the fields of self-healing and self-transformation. He explains that words are crystallized thoughts and have life-changing power when spoken with conviction, concentration, willpower, and feeling. Yogananda offers far more than mere suggestions for achieving positive attitudes. He shows how to impregnate words with spiritual force to shift habitual thought patterns of the mind and create a new personal reality.

Added to this text are over fifty of Yogananda's well-loved "Short Affirmations," taken from issues of *East-West* and *Inner Culture* magazines from 1932 to 1942. This little book will be a treasured companion on the road to realizing your highest, divine potential.

METAPHYSICAL MEDITATIONS
Paramhansa Yogananda

Metaphysical Meditations is a classic collection of meditation techniques, visualizations, affirmations, and prayers from the great yoga master, Paramhansa Yogananda. The meditations given are of three types: those spoken to the individual consciousness, prayers or demands addressed to God, and affirmations that bring us closer to the Divine.

Select a passage that meets your specific need and speak each word slowly and purposefully until you become absorbed in its inner meaning. At the bedside, by the meditation seat, or while traveling—one can choose no better companion than *Metaphysical Meditations*.

KARMA AND REINCARNATION
The Wisdom of Yogananda, Volume 2

Yogananda reveals the reality of karma, death, reincarnation, and the afterlife. With clarity and simplicity, he makes the mysterious understandable: why we see a world of suffering and inequality; what happens at death and after death; the purpose of reincarnation; and how to handle the challenges we face in our lives.

MOMENTS OF TRUTH, VOLUME ONE
Excerpts from *The Rubaiyat of Omar Khayyam Explained*
Paramhansa Yogananda

Moments of Truth, Volume One is the first in a series of small books of excerpts from the teachings of Paramhansa Yogananda, as set forth in his own books and in those of his close disciple, Swami Kriyananda.

The gems of wisdom in this little volume are taken from Yogananda's commentaries on *The Rubaiyat of Omar Khayyam*, considered by Westerners a celebration of earthly pleasures, but widely recognized in the East as a work of profound spirituality. Yogananda's commentaries are a true scripture in their own right. These selections have scripture's power to change your consciousness, and your life.

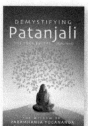

DEMYSTIFYING PATANJALI: THE YOGA SUTRAS
The Wisdom of Paramhansa Yogananda
Presented by his direct disciple, Swami Kriyananda

For millennia this fascinating series of yoga sutras, or aphorisms, by the great Indian sage Patanjali has baffled scholars and mystics alike. Today, these powerful writings stand newly revealed as a practical, concise handbook that redirects all sincere seekers swiftly towards their true home in the Divine.

Demystifying Patanjali represents the confluence of three great yoga teachers. Patanjali, the first exponent of the ancient teachings of yoga, presented his system of inner contemplation, meditation practice, and ethics. Paramhansa Yogananda, perhaps the greatest of all yoga masters to live and teach in the West, revealed with deep insight the meaning behind Patanjali's often obscure aphorisms. Finally, Yogananda's direct disciple, Swami Kriyananda, the author of nearly 150 spiritual books in his own right, compiled his guru's explanation into a clear, systematic presentation.

These three great souls combine to give us a modern scripture that will enlighten the mind, expand the heart, and inspire the soul of every seeker.

THE ESSENCE OF THE BHAGAVAD GITA

Explained by Paramhansa Yogananda
As remembered by his disciple, Swami Kriyananda

Rarely in a lifetime does a new spiritual classic appear that has the power to change people's lives and transform future generations. This is such a book. This revelation of India's best-loved scripture approaches it from a fresh perspective, showing its deep allegorical meaning and down-to-earth practicality. The themes presented are universal: how to achieve victory in life through union with the Divine; how to prepare for life's final exam—death—and what happens afterward; and how to triumph over all pain and suffering.

Swami Kriyananda worked with Paramhansa Yogananda in 1950 while the Master completed his commentary. At that time, Yogananda commissioned him to disseminate his teachings worldwide.

"Millions will find God through this book!" Yogananda declared upon completion of the manuscript. "Not just thousands—millions. I have seen it. I know."

STORIES FROM INDIA, VOLUME 1
First in the Wisdom Stories series
Paramhansa Yogananda

This treasury of Indian tales will delight both the casual reader and students of Eastern thought. Featuring a gamut of characters—from saints to thieves, God-realized masters to lions and frogs—these stories were all told by Paramhansa Yogananda in his lectures, informal talks, and writings.

Yogananda knew that stories have a way of bringing out a childlike openness within us, regardless of our age. In that openness, heart and mind make connections the intellect alone might miss. He told these tales to illustrate the spiritual and practical truths he was teaching.

It is not enough to be inspired by spiritual truths. We must be able to apply those teachings to our daily lives.

Each story is followed by a "wisdom gem," illuminating spiritually vital topics such as right action, courage, unconditional love, faith, and wisdom—an enjoyable way to explore and reflect on these universal qualities. For ease of use, the stories are indexed by the qualities they illustrate. Whether you are a teacher, parent, student, or devotee, these stories are an excellent resource to turn to again and again for inspiration, sharing, and personal study.

YOUR SUN SIGN AS A SPIRITUAL GUIDE

Swami Kriyananda

Swami Kriyananda shows how, with awareness, attention, and will, one can cultivate the higher potential of a person's sign rather than being limited by its karmic energy, leading to greater fulfillment and success. The horoscope shows karmic patterns of energy. We can learn to work with these energies and develop their more refined, higher octaves, which will then magnetize new possibilities into our lives.

This book also guides the seeker to an understanding of the subtle aspects of the spiritual path as it manifests for him through his particular sun sign. Yogic understanding is rich and often runs counter to prevailing thought. So too with astrology, the reader will find vistas of understanding opening as he takes the words and guidance of this yogic view of astrology to heart. This book reassures the reader that sun-sign weaknesses can be spiritual strengths if pursued rightly. It also warns one not to rest on the laurels of sun-sign strengths, but to go much deeper. Concentrated, deep wisdom is available to the seeker in this brief, easy-to-digest book that helps the reader to understand himself and others from a higher perspective.

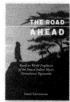

THE ROAD AHEAD
Based on World Prophecies of the Famed
Indian Mystic Paramhansa Yogananda
Swami Kriyananda

If ever there was a time when the future of the human race was in doubt, it is now. More and more reputable economists are predicting worldwide depression. Dwindling sources of energy threaten dire shortages of many of the prime necessities of modern life.

Whatever the future holds in store for us, one thing is certain: We may look forward to sweeping changes in our lives in the years to come.

Based on the predictions that Paramhansa Yogananda made not to frighten us, but to strengthen us to deal with what lies ahead. Even suffering has its divine purpose: changing harmful habits that keep us imprisoned in lower consciousness. The best preparation of all is to deepen our inner life and attune our individual will with the will of God. Those who do so will come out of this period stronger and freer.

The Road Ahead can be our road map. It shows us how to move forward through the challenges and obstacles in our path toward new horizons of greater spiritual awareness and unity for humanity as a whole.

GOD AS DIVINE MOTHER
Wisdom and Inspiration for Love and Acceptance
Paramhansa Yogananda and *Swami Kriyananda*

We long for a God who loves us exactly as we are, who doesn't judge us but rather helps and encourages us in achieving our highest potential. In this book, discover the teachings and inspirations on Divine Mother from Paramhansa Yogananda. These teachings are universal: No matter your religious background, or lack thereof, you will find these messages of love and acceptance resonating on a soul-level. Included also are over thirty poems and prayers dedicated to God in the form of Divine Mother, and original chants and songs by the authors.

"The role of the Divine Mother is to draw all Her children, all self-aware beings everywhere, back to oneness with God."

In this book, you will discover: Who is Divine Mother?; How to develop the heart's natural love; What attitudes draw Her grace; How to tune in to Divine Mother. Included also are over thirty poems and prayers dedicated to God in the form of Divine Mother, as well as original chants and songs by the authors.

For more titles in books, audibooks, spoken word, music, and videos, and for a complete cataolgue of Crystal Clarity Publishers products, visit **crystalclarity.com**